MOWING LEAVES OF GRASS

by

MATT SEDILLO

FLOWERSONG
PRESS

Mowing Leaves of Grass

Matt Sedillo

FLOWERSONG
P R E S S

FlowerSong Press
McAllen, Texas 78501

Copyright © 2019 by Matt Sedillo

ISBN: 978-1-7338092-9-0

Published by FlowerSong Press
in the United States of America.
www.flowersongbooks.com

Mowing Leaves of Grass first published in *Cultural Weekly* October 9th, 2019
Kingdom of Cages originally published in *LA Taco* December 5th, 2018

Set in Adobe Garamond Pro

Cover design and typeset by Matthew Revert

For my mom, who took me to libraries since before I can remember.

Foreword

How do you decolonize classroom curriculum when the status quo is dependent on blurring fact and fiction? Matt Sedillo exposes the lies that obscure the barbaric, dehumanizing actions of the ruling class that have a stronghold on the worldview of right and wrong. His words are unapologetic truth; powerful and seemingly harsh, but ultimately transformative, rooted in love and urgency. I delight in his ability to accurately indict the evils in this world without so much as a flinch or a second guess. Each of his poems are socio-economic and political discourse wrapped up in the epitome of literary excellence. I believe all social justice educators, and above all, Ethnic Studies scholar warriors, should use this collection to critically illuminate their curriculum.

Matt Sedillo introduced me to the concept of the "three act poem" when he came to work with my students in South Central Los Angeles and also when he offered a workshop to liberation educators at the Association of Raza Educators Statewide Conference in 2019. The "three act poem" is his gift to poets, scholars and liberation activists alike, for it does not stop at calling out oppression in witty eye-opening metaphoric detail, but is simultaneously a call to action that speaks truth to power. It's powerful to witness young poets invigorated with the tool of counter-narrative ethnography embedded in the "three act poem" that allows them to become eloquent storytellers and activist organizers at the same time. The truth can be said of his power to sharpen the skills of seasoned poets by reminding them of the power in their words to start a revolution and transform the world.

Matt's book of poetry is a great tool for teachers to use for its historical references; the first two poems alone allude to countless historical deletions and/or deceptions of history in the American education system, such as, "…housing covenants that greeted great migrations and did the same to the Mexicans." This book is tremendously useful to use as a supplement for any lesson worthy of being called critical. In fact, every one of the poems can be used to formulate lessons that "critique empire and its relationship to white supremacy, racism, patriarchy, cisheteropatriarchy, capitalism, ableism, anthropocentrism, and other forms of power and oppression at the intersections of our society." I highly recommend that all critical educators employ not just the content of "Mowing Leaves of Grass" in their classrooms but also Matt Sedillo's dialectical understanding of Pedagogy of the Oppressed.

This book needs to become the Holy Writ of scholar guerrerx activists, transformative decolonial educators, righteous contrarian poets, students in need of cultivating their roots (ripe for uprooting the oppressive contradictions that plague them), and everyone's abuelit@!

In solidarity,
Guadalupe Carrasco Cardona
Association of Raza Educators, Los Angeles

Table of Contents

Pilgrim

See, some were born to summer homes
And palatial groves
Where pain was only to ever unfold
From the pages of Secret Gardens
Where the Red Fern Grows
But not I
See, I come from the stock
Of starry-eyed astronauts
Who greet the night sky
With big dreams and wide eyes
Always Running
Down the Devil's Highway
Through Occupied America
On the way back to
The House on Mango Street
And all those other books
You didn't want us to read
Raised on handball
Off the back wall
Of a panaderia
Born
East the river
Post Mendez vs Westminster
One generation removed
From the redlines
And diplomas signed

That those dreams
In that skin
Need not apply
See, I come from struggle
And if my story offends you
That is only 'cause you made the mistake of seeking your
reflection
In my self-portrait
See, this
Well this may not be about you
Because while some were born
To the common core
Whose reflected faces
Graced the pages
Of doctrines to discover
And ages to be explored
Where old world hardships
Crashed against new shores
New England
New Hampshire
New Jersey
New York
For others pushed off
Turtle island
Aztlan
Do not call this brown skin immigrant
Child of the sun
Son of the conquest
Mexicano blood

Running through the veins
Of the eastside of Los Angeles
Do not tell him
In what native tongue
His song would best be sung
Do not tell me
Who I am
'Cause I was raised just like you
Miseducated in some of those
Very same schools
Off lessons and legends
Of honest injuns and Christian pilgrims
And a nation of immigrants
All united in freedom
That is until they pulled aside
My white friend
Pointed directly at me
And said "Scott
I judge you by the company you keep
And you spend your time with this"
And that's the same old story since 1846
The adventures of Uncle Sam
The stick-up man
Hey wetback
Show me your papers
Now give me your labor
The Melting Pot
Was never meant for the hands
That clean it

The American dream
Has always come at the expense
Of those who tucked it in
And you don't know that
'Cause you don't teach it
Could write you a book
But you won't read it
So you know what
This is about you
And 1492
And the treaty of Guadalupe
California missions
And Arizona schools
And these racists
That try to erase us
As we raise their kids
In cities that bear our names
But you're going to learn
Something today
'Cause from Ferdinand
To minuteman
From Arpaio
To Alamo
From Popol Vuh
To Yo Soy Joaquin
To the Indian that still lives in me
From Mexico 68
To the missing 43
They tried to bury us

They didn't know we were seeds
From Cananea mine
To Delano strike
From the Plan De Ayala
Emiliano Zapata
Joaquin Murrieta
Las Adelitas
Brown Berets
And Zapatistas
From Richard Nixon
To the Third Napoleon
From Peckinpah
To Houston
From Lone Star Republic
To Christopher Columbus
All the way down
To Donald fucking Trump
We didn't cross the borders
The borders crossed us
Who you calling immigrant
Pilgrim?

Stolen Lives, Stolen Land

Sundown, Levittown
Fort Apache, Dirty Harry
John Wayne, Blackface
Minuteman, Moynihan
Gone with the Wind, Breaking Bad
Washington Redskin, Confederate Flag
The sword, the dollar
The cannon, the scholar
The Cavalry and the Ivy League
History as written by lightning
Is the rising smoke of burning village
The ways and means by which victors keep their victims
A Frontier Thesis
Some Notes on the State of Virginia
Extraction, expansion
The Winning of the West
Lewis and Clark, Smith and Wesson
Now circle the wagon with bloodshed and slaves' sweat
The crack of the whip, the law of three-fifths
The crowned republic of King Cotton
The intended failures of reconstruction
The housing covenants that greeted great migrations and did
the same to the Mexicans
And poor Mexico, so far from heaven and so close to Monroe
Doctrine, to Davey Crocket
To prison industrial complex

A war on drugs is a war on our young
Bloody Christmas, Reefer Madness, fifteen to life for four ounces
East Oakland, West Baltimore
South of La Brea and Oliver North
Plymouth Rock, Jamestown and the Rio Grande
Stolen lives, stolen land

The Devil

You see
I heard
It said somewhere
That there's a sucker born
Every minute
And I am just here
To provide a service
Get them on their way
Get them
Custom fitted
And they say it's like
Stealing candy
From a baby
But it's more like
Selling crack to a fiend
Bieber to a tween
A winning Nigerian lottery ticket to a fool
Tom Cruise to a desperate housewife
Or Scientology
To Tom Cruise
Yes you see there is a sucker
Born every minute
And I'm just here to let them know they got some options
Coke or Pepsi
Ford or Chevy
Adidas or Nike

A Mac or a PC
A college education
Or a reverse mortgage
Get them knee-deep
In the blood of the Congolese
In Indonesian sweat
Or just good old-fashioned American debt
Don't like the way I do business
Go ahead then
Organize
Occupy
Protest
Start a boycott
I'll just hire a PR firm
Reorganize my sweatshops
Restructure your loan
Then auction you
Out of house and home
I am the American way
I am your raised flag
Now pledge allegiance
And they say
It's like stealing candy
From a baby
But it's more like
Stealing an election
Starting a war
On a false pretense
Giving the contracts

To my friends
Then reviewing my stock options
I am the cross-section
Of business
And politics
I am a Washington lobbyist
I am Jack Abramoff
Fred Thompson
Dick Cheney
And you had best pay me
I am the reason
Why you can't fight city hall
But I can buy
A Supreme Court justice
For the fainthearted
Those born of weak stomach
I am corruption
But for those
Bold
Enough to call the Devil
Out by his name
I answer to capitalism
And I run shit
And I heard
There was a sucker born
Every minute
And I am just here
To provide a service
Give them something to believe in

So I am the opiate of the masses
I am that
Christian Zionist
Picking your pocket
Painting pictures
Of Armageddon
Pocketing a percentage
Then sending the rest
To the IDF
To gun down some Palestinians
I am organized religion
A scandal
Brewing in the Vatican
A Wahhabist
On the payroll
Of a Saudi Prince
A Hindu nationalist
Calling for ethnic cleansing
And purification
I am Pat fucking Robertson
All up in your airwaves
Calling for political assassination
I am a holy man
A man of the cloth
And I wrap myself
In holy garbs
Wash the blood
From my hands
And watch

The money roll in
I am a businessman
I am the poor you shall always have
I am what Caesar takes
Whether or not
You are willing to give it
I am the divine right of kings
I am he who shall not work
Shall not eat
And we are not hiring
Go die
I am every side
Of every coin
I am feudalism
I am slavery
I am the free market
I am the one percent
I am capitalism
And I will watch your children starve
To satisfy my greed
I am the mark
Of the beast
And I ride
On war
Famine
Genocide
And the bottom line
I am the motherfucking devil
And I run shit
What the fuck you gonna do about it?

The Census

It happened fast
It happened young
A song
Nestled in your ear
A psalm of forgetting
A hymn of daggers and fog
Neither here nor there
You were taught
You embodied nowhere
Now declare your voice absent
Bow your head
And present your palms
You happened gray
You happened odd
No one
From nowhere
Born forgotten
The moral of your story
Quickly discarded
The invisible backs
That move the market
Now back to work
And thank the bosses
'Cause nothing ever changes
But the census
Spic
Hispanic

Speak English wetback

Dirty

Stupid

Lazy

Good for nothing

Job stealing

Mexican

UnAmerican

Invasion by birth canal

Born of a nation of mongrels

Not far removed from the mountains

See how fast that happens

Once

Once upon a dream
Or at least so I heard
From the time long before
In a land now distant
We gathered
Took shelter from the winter
Our child eyes
One with the stars
Collected moonbeams
Our veins, rivers and streams
Our heart was a beat
And each generation
One to the next
We built stronger nests
And legends
Were left
Fuller than found
Or at least so I heard
From the time
Before
I was born on a stretch of land
Known for its weather
Where
The sun shone its light
Upon the righteous and the wicked
The wretched and the privileged

The innocent and truly guilty alike
As their gilded steps
Fell upon our heads
For those who own the land own the law
And those who do not
Only its consequence
I had this dream once
A man walked a child
To the edge of a hill
Upon which sat a mansion
He pointed up and said "son
There live the rich
And though you and I
May never live to see it
One day this hill will run red with their blood"
Sometimes I have all the strength
And sometimes I have none at all
I have this recurring life
Where every moment is midnight
And every step is fog
Wake up
Wake up
Wake up on downtown bus ride
Alongside
A friend of mine
Tell me your troubles
I'll tell you mine
Or we can just shoot the breeze
Pass the time

Something about a job
Something about the car
Some run in with the cops
How I almost got fucked up by the law
How everyone just stood around
And watched
How I talked my way out
Like I usually do
Tells me school kids
Are chanting in her children's face
"Trump"
"Trump"
And "Build the wall"
We were children during prop 187
This is worse
I imagine
I pause
I restart
This is worse I know
It ebbs and it flows
Always really coming
And it never really goes
How our kids are never just kids
In this country
We talk history
Mendez and Lemon Grove
Rodriguez vs San Antonio
Saul Castro and the blowouts
McGraw Hill and Texas

How Tucson unified against us
How our ancestors walk with us
How our legends rattle our bones
How la lucha makes us strong
But la luna makes us who we are
She tells me she doesnt like to ride the bus alone
At least not at night
Tells me of dangers
I never have to consider
How the world is full of threat
Because the world is full of men
No exceptions
I sit
I listen
The wheels keep turning
We reach our destination
Walk our separate ways
I find no peace these days
I head east
Towards clinics of cruelty
All humanity stripped from a system
Sadism posed as social work
In El Monte
The writing on the wall
Will insult you in two languages
On the corner
Of Paramount and Whittier
On the border
Of Montebello and Pico Rivera

Signs ring out to criminalize our movement
Six months in a cage for cruising
My father always said
They hate to see us shining
The car was once his
Its days are few
My feet are weary
I sleep in parking lots
Sleepwalk my way
To the westside
Some kind of festival of lights
At the edge of conquest
At the beginning or end
Of the Christopher Columbus highway
I make my way
Waist deep to the pacific
I welcome the waves
Make distant the land
Make distant its chant
Come this far to forget
Feel the moonlight ripple my skin
Awake again
I walk the pier
See them in the distance
The boys in blue
The killing crew
Authorized lynch mob
Death squad
America signed with a bullet

Five pigs to one teenager
Hands cuffed behind his back
Loud proud frat boys walk by
Drinking from flasks
Black youth is criminalized
White crime
Is state sanctioned
The guns
Their triggers
Their laughter
They call for back up
No crowd gathers
The city's eyes
The city's lights
March forward
This is expected
This is nothing to see
This what we have come to imagine
Never once
In all their murderous authority
Do they ever stop laughing
After an hour
They release him
No explanation
They simply
Tell him to stay out of trouble
This is the law of the land
I have this dream
Every so often

Of people
Beyond borders and prisons
Gathered in the distance
Telling tales of a time
When women feared the evening
When communities were punished by color
And grown men hunted children
Hardly able to believe
People once lived this way

Raise the Red Flag

They say freedom isn't free
But neither is a tank of gasoline
John McCain was tortured for someone's sins
But not mine
US proletariat
Self-taught Marxist
Organic Chicano intellect
Bound in contradiction
Born in the belly of the beast
Many things
But the wind beneath the wing
Of a war machine
Never
And you can spend your whole life
Throwing pebbles at a glass ceiling
Only to discover it was the bottom of a shark tank
But you knew that
And I didn't come to make friends
And I didn't come to hold hands
I came to talk shit
Raise the red flag
See whose still with me
George Clooney
Salma Hayek
Angelina Jolie
Don Cheadle

National Petroluem Radio
MSDNC
Brian Williams said the bombs were beautiful
The obliterator of nations
Hillary Clinton rushing from her silence
Demanding more bloodshed
Antonio
Julian
Joaquin
What a blessing
To see my reflection
In all this murder and mayhem
Bono and Oprah
Trudeua and Obama
America Ferrera
Farheed Zakariah
Take up the neoliberal burden
The rainbow coalition of death
And I didn't come to make friends
And I didn't come to hold hands
I came to talk shit
Raise the red flag
See whose still with me

#fakenewscoup

The fire the fury a wall like never seen
A tariff, a tweet
Stacks of paper with nothing printed on breadcrumbs
A press conference coup
The paper tiger unfolds
The empire has no clothes
Carnival barker runs out of options
The opposition does not have
The military the legislation
And most importantly
They do not have the people
And here comes Trumpty Dumpty
Tweeting at four am again
Covfefe

The Servant's Song

Thrones of blood
Thrones of blood
Empires of sweat
Chambers of commerce
Ministers of finance
Columns of debt
The law is print
Its right is script
High priests
Preach the evangelical
Cannons aim steady
The doctrine of famine and luxury
War is progress
Property is sacred
Starvation is the market
Your mouths are reckless
Look at the gates
They are blood-ready
Captains of industry
Lords of limited liability
Well-dressed murderous thieves
The modern kings of corporate speech
Walk among us
As loaded guns
Chambers locked
Full of legal teams

Legalese
And just enough
Finely
Printed
Legal degrees
Of separation
To wash their teeth clean
Predators in every sense of the word
It is a wolves run
The night
Capitalists
Gather around a bonfire
To listen
To the servant's song
"How vain are we
How vain are we
Us composed of cosmic dust
Set beneath the stars
To chart
Out our brief chaotic lives
By the time
It takes our small fragile distant eyes"
To finally
See the light
Praise be the sky
Praise be the day
And praise be the night
With your steps moonlit
Press your face to the wind

Let the harvest
Drink you in
Blessed
Be our lungs
Oh how our lungs have blessed us
Your body
Conduit
Between breath and the divine
Praise be the vine
Praise be the joy it brings to your eyes
At this both guests and host were pleased
At servant
Clever and observant
Unburdened
By the groundbreaking decisions
That set the shoulders of titans
And who better
Than one given to a life of service
To serve as reminder
To breath easy
"How forgetful are we
How forgetful are we
Our tongues dripping
Tripping
Over one another
To touch up monuments
Climb ladders of success
Deliver the speech
Of self-made men

Oh how we forget
The very soil
We walk upon
Has been toiled by many hands
That even the tree's tallest branch
Grew from the same seed
As the root"
At this
Both guests and hosts were amused
At a servant
Humble yet with sense of purpose
And who better
Than one given to a life of service
To serve as reminder
Of the divine order
Of all things
"How tragic are we
How tragic
Indeed
Our whole lives boulders and mountains
And the drive
To make sense of them
Oceans to conquer
Soil to bleed
And to each
A plot of sun
A job to be done
Please
Please

As we
As we push this rock together
Do not strike at us
So mercilessly"
At this
Neither guests nor hosts were pleased
The night had become political
For what good is a servant
Whose demands exceed their purpose
The capitalists cried out
"Have we not been good to you
Have we not given you all that you have
And in all your years of service
Have you not heard
Have you not learned
The law
Is threat
Its right
Is death
Look at the gates
Supreme justice
Reigns upon us"
In the servant's quarters
The servant's daughter
Sings a different song
One of blood and conquest
Fire and vengeance
Dawn and the horizon
Of a new day rising

Dreams of hacienda burning
Reads
Of the gallows
The guillotine
Firing squads
And basements full of Romanovs
She laughs
She weeps
She dreams
She speaks
With the others
And with each passing day
They grow strong

Defend the Eastside

The 5
The 101
The 10
Suavecito for president
A funeral procession
Out of City Terrace
No ICE on the overpass
Just a shot
On the countertop
Next to
Hot chilaquiles
No liquor license needed
Just a morning prayer for the dead
Just a few words for the old man
So raise your glass
To the 60
Atlantic
And the 710
To watching
Semillas grow
Through strollers
Through Los Puntos
A brick
Through gentrified windows
All the better
To die on your feet

'Cause life's a risk
A wedding dress
Off Whittier
A baptism
At our lady
A reception
At La Raza
At the intersection
Of Mission
And Disobey Trump
In the shadow
Of Zapata
Better late than never
My love
Will we be
Standing here
In fifty years?
Like fire and memory
There are things
Worth protecting
Like imagine
Long
After I am gone
And the children grown
Corazon at Mariachi
Watching kids flip ollies
Over burning effigies
Of America's
Latest flaming racist

Like we did
When our love was young
When our eyes were locked
When our hands were bonds
You will remember me
Driving the 60
The 5
The 710
But will this world still exist?
This life as lived
Like fire and memory
Like all that is worth protecting
Defend the eastside

Carved Over

Draw a map
Line the sand
Carve the desert
Act on land
Amend it
Eminent domain
Indefinite detention
Private prisons
Public referendum
Gentrification
Naturalization
Americanization
Forced sterilization
Make America Great Again
Mexico will pay
The hunt for Murrieta
The hunt for Pancho Villa
John Pershing's slaughter of the innocents
A severed head
Touring California museums
Becomes Zorro
Becomes the Wild Bunch
Becomes whitewash
This American Life
Experience
Its imagination

If you can dream it
You can see it
And if you can see it
You can build it
And if you build it
You can take it
And if they resist
Manifest a cruelty
So complete
That for generations
They will do it to themselves
Build a city
Draw its borders
Patrol its districts
Add silence to injury
Insult without memory
Protect these borders
From language and culture
Taco trucks
And Dora the Explorer
The country is changing
And you know it
It's simple mathematics
And you know it
You have kept us weak
By keeping us confused
Your grandchildren
Will speak Spanglish
In the neighborhood

You grew up in
Greeting their friends
On the corner
Of your childhood
And cherished memories
Under the lamplight
And faded midst
This historic site
Of your first kiss
Where you learned
To sink
Before you learned to swim
Where you
And she
Carved your names to trees
And promised each other
Forever
But
Memories fade
Neighborhoods change
And your names will be carved over
And there is nothing
You can do about it
And you know this too
So when Donald Trump
Says drug dealers and rapists
And Kelly Osbourne jumps in
To correct him
No Donald

Those people are just here to clean our shit
When you
Sit so comfortably
Speak so freely
About a group of people
Who are somehow everywhere
Yet at the same time
No one
Hold your tongue
We are far closer than you know

Pedagogy of the Oppressor

And when they read
They read in conquest
And when they thought
They thought of process
And when they wrote
Again and again
It was the word progress
And when they spoke
A festival of bayonets
Impaled the audience
Line the children
It's getting late November
Teach them Pilgrim
Teach them Indian
Speak of gratitude
Speak of friendship

Chicano Bros in Jaguar Suits

Memes schemes
Group messaging
Committees
Ad hoc
Collectivize shit-talk
Heard the house cat
Laugh the second
Fall of Tenochtitlan
Draw
Silly Mexican gallos
In feathers speaking foolish
Challenge
Chicano bros in
Jaguar suits
To a response
Self-lightening grinch who stole poetry
The scourge of teacher collectives
The forty-something year old schoolyard bully
There are builders and then there are wreckers
I would name you
But wouldn't want to make you famous
My shit talk is immortal
You're a footnote at best

Wagon's Thread

Filtered through pavement
The citizens
Civilian
Of conquest
Pour in
Little products
Into little boxes
Where buffalo
Once danced
And humans once being
Now citizens
Civilized
Fed
But not free
Now pay toll
To pavement
Littered
Glittering
Strip malls
And city lights
Monuments
And copyright
Anthems
And allegiance
Denial and disconnect
The threat

Is not external
It is stitched
To the wagon's thread
To nightmare
And to national skin
A house
On a hill
A home on a range
Call it safe
Raise a flag
Load a gun
Build a gate
The blood
On our hands
The scars
On our backs
Our minds alone
Prisoners
Of a past
That has not yet past
And everywhere
There is war
Fog lifts
Lady Liberty
Dust kicks
Manifest destiny
Picket fence
White flight
And the model minority

The suburbs
Are a dream
Within a dream
Within a dream
An America
Within America
Within America
At your feet
The apartments
Above you
Rolling hills of privilege
Been a long time
Since those rabbits
Chased after carrots
Life
Liberty
And the pursuit
Of inheritance
But deep down
You know
These colors do run
And the paint does crack
And though it may be a long
Way down
It's just a short road back
So work yourself
To ulcer
At the altar
Of appearances

You earned this
Deserve this
Make
Religion of it
More than a conqueror
You were born to be prosperous
Shining and magnificent
You are the Joneses
Now circle this wagon
And protect
This fortress
Rally
For safer communities
For SB1070
For minimum sentencing
For prop 187
For gang injunction
For three strike law
For neighborhood watch
For stand your ground
Stand over graveyards
In shock and awe
Through blood and dust
Through steel and rust
Of what we have become
Of where we have been
Of what we are born
Little products
In front of little boxes

Filtered through
All the news fit to print
Blissful and ignorant
Now stay in tune
With your television set
Vote
Against Willie Horton
Vote
Against illegal immigrant
Vote
Against teachers' union
Vote
Against your own self-interest
This
Will keep you safe
Race
And illusion
State
And confusion
Frontiers
Are not freedom
A fortress
Is a prison
The air is toxic
The water is poisoned
The suburbs
Are filled
With asbestos
This is not good for you

This has made you hateful
This house
Is a caged fever
A night terror
The bloody drone
The rising smoke
The ocean
White with foam
Far and safe
From anywhere
The lit night sky
Tears flesh
From bone
America
The only home
I have ever known
America
The only home
I have ever known
America
The only home
I have ever known
And everywhere
This flag is flown
There is war

Shithole/Triumph of the Deal

Three words
Closed circuit television
Invest in drones
For your family's protection
This place is becoming a real shithole
Three of my neighbors
Don't even speak English
Well they do
Over the fence
But when they go inside
I can hear them
And sometimes
More of them come over
Parking near my house
Carrying boxes
Holding children
Looking just like them
The smell of food
The sound of music
What's going on in there
And other times
Late at night
When I review my videos
I can see the police

Just showing up at their houses
And I can't even tell why
Looked like
They were just sitting in their car
Looked like
They were just walking to their door
Sounds like
I am not getting the full story here
'Cause I know
Some of these kids
Will grow to be men
And that's a direct threat
And the others
Women
Who I do not trust
They might laugh at me yuck
What are they saying?
What are they thinking?
That's not even English
This isn't fair
I am the real victim here
Don't look in my direction
Don't tread on my lawn
In the name of Donald Trump
And Roseanne Barr
I am going to march
To the edge of my property
Defend my country
This land that I love

My fence is White
Jesus is White
Santa is White
Megyn Kelly is White
Ivanka is White
Elvis Presley is White
America is White
White
White
White
White
White
White
Taylor Swift is White
Look what you made me do
Not far from here
Not far at all really
There was a town
Beautiful town
Then but
Now I am getting ahead of myself
There was a hill
A winning hill just magnificent
A beautiful hill
Believe me
This was back
When we sat
In the driver's seat
Of the winning team

Ate from daddy's plate
Drank big milk
In the winner's circle
At the winter games
And in the autumn
Summer and spring
We were winners too
I love winning
I hate losing
That's why I never
Do it was the kind of hill
You would want to build a town on
But you couldn't
There was already one there
Are you even paying attention?
High on a hill
Overlooking a valley
Lush and green
With wells, aqueducts
Humble people and wheat
Where the town got its meat
And oh this town butchers
Stupendous
And oh this towns bakers
Tremendous
The town smelled terrific
Pick an adjective
This town was it
And could it run

Its mechanics
Its lawyers
Its locksmiths
Their doctors
And accountants
They were killers
Believe me
In those days
We were smart
In those days
We were tough
And we built things
We don't build things anymore
Everything is built somewhere else
Sad
And everyone is scared
Scared of what?
Of saying there's a problem
I am not scared
There's a problem
Of saying where it came from
We all know
Down in the valley
Dirty
Breeding
Ungrateful
Infestation
Shithole
Animals

Yes animals
I said it
Now you can too
So a man rose above the town
And half the town pretended to hate him
And half the town pretended
Not to know where he came from
The fair-haired son
Of their proud blood
He crushed the enemy
Opened the flood
For soil and blood
Left no child behind
Each and every one torn
From eyes and arms
Like all who had come before him
And the town turned away
Knowing it had to be done
You see this was the most magnificent
Beautiful
Excellent
Exquisite
Elegant
Winning
Shining city on a hill
The greatest town
The world had ever known
Believe me

La Reina

Los Angeles
Is full of abuelas
Who raise grandkids in Spanglish
Under the watchful eye
Of Cuactemoc the Virgin and Jesus
Make a village out of a duplex
Raised Catholic
But the roots are indigenous
Several generations
Of family extension
All growing in one plot
Hand-me-downs
Under shared roofs, rooms and reflections
In Lak'ech
Por que mi casa es tu casa
And that's not empty promises
That's family living
That's palabra
So light a candle
Burn some sage
Pick your saints
And set your altar
The sign of the cross
The sound of the conch
And prayers lift
To the four directions

And that's culture
Not contradiction
Folks in the back
They fight for a living
Fight for fifteen
Hail from the rowdy section
Of Dodger's Stadium
But their hearts still burn
With the fire
From that Chavez Ravine
And here is home of La Reina
At fifty-four cents on the dollar
America's most exploited worker
Neglected
Disrespected
Underrepresented
Presumed incompetent
If she lives life as expected she will be labeled statistic
If she manages to outpace them
Threatened
They will blame affirmative action
But either way
They will not see her
They will demand her labor
Paid and unpaid smiling
Her eyes humble
And her mouth silent
Lady of the river
City's past present and future

The queen of angels
Invisible to those
Who float
Through canyons lagoons and cemeteries
Whitewashing adobe
Through a series of fevered dreams
Connected by a bridge called her back
To those who make demands
To the stories told to bury the past
To the ones that serve to remind her
That she works for them
That she is lucky
To even have a job
Here in El Pueblo
De Nuestra Senora
La Reina
De los angeles
Del Rio Porcincula
Or as they like to call it
LA LA land
In the 1780s we built a pueblo
In the 1890s in the brickyards of Montebello
We built one again
Only to be beaten and shot
Only for no Mexicans no dogs
Only for a different set of rules
For a different set of schools
Only to be written out of the history
Of a city

We founded
As we are priced out of the homes
Of our mothers
As more and more
Of greater Los Angeles
Is suddenly discovered
And this is the struggle of our forebearers
One para pan historia y tierra
Hasta la victoria siempre
The struggle is real
La lucha sigue
Y La Reina
De Los Angeles
Is on the frontlines
Of every fight
Holding it down
Holding up the better half of the sky
Fighting gentrification
Fighting for education
Fighting for tenants' rights
Fighting la migra y la jura
'Cause fuck the police
Y chinga la ICE
Fight for dignity hers and ours
All the damn time
Proud and brown
And brown and proud
Are the hearts and hands
The backbone of these raised fists

So when we throw two fingers up
When we say fuck Donald Trump
That's not identity politics
That's the cry of the proletariat
And at fifty-four cents on the dollar
She is the face of it
So when you see her
When you see her
Pushing some other mother's stroller
Locked behind cash registers
Coming off that third, fourth, fifth shift of the oppressed
Show some respect
Bow your head
And bend the knee
All hail La Reina
The once and future queen

And If

We don't pay dues
We start unions
We don't need a PR campaign
We are the people's movement
And if revolution is an art
Then let these streets be our canvases
And if injustice has an arc
Then let this poem
Be known as a stone thrown to shatter it
Scatter the city planners' future to the wind
Make war on everyday genocide
Disturb the peace of empire
Permits we don't need no stinking permits?
In the hillside village
Just steps from my childhood home
The branches of a tree
Crumble a brick wall
And if that doesn't tell you something

Oh Say

Heart in hand
Heart in hand
My eyes
Stretched the perilous sky
And oh say
What did they see?
My feet
Never reached
Any purple mountain's majesty
But my ears
My ears have kissed the tongue
Of that revivalist thump
From
Gettysburg
To the Mason-Dixon
Where the Civil War
Never ended
And Lincoln
Never lived
At least not as it was written
In histories
Never learned
So we were bound
To repeat them
In histories
Never learned

So we were bound

To keep singing

Oh captain

My captain

Drunk on blood anthems

Blind patriots

Raised flags

And fallen veterans

The myths

The hymns

The bitterness

Of fairy tales

Best woven into song

From the dawn's

Early light

To twilight's last gleaming

From Plymouth Rock

To Dred Scott

From smallpox

To church bomb

From black bodies

Swinging in the summer breeze

To the endless blood

Of countless wounded knees

Old glory

We are born

Witness

To the sins of your soil

Oh pioneer

Rich
Off that manifest
Off that go west
That gold coast
That gold rush
All that gold dust
Off all
That California dreams are made of
All made to play a part
To sing along
To hum a bar
In thanksgiving
Of that genocide opera
Oh say
Can you feel it?
The birth of a nation
Redlines and segregation
Boarding schools and reservations
Mexican kids beaten in class
For speaking Spanish
The Lakota forced to pray Christian
Western civilization
Is citizen fiction
White hats
White men
And sunsets
Walter White
How much Mexican bloodshed
For one hour

Of conquest entertainment?
Oh melting pot
How these bones
Have grown
In that hellish kitchen
Of that marrow-shaking tribalism
Of that Ellis Island
Of your George M. Cohan
Of your Don Corleone
Of your Yankee Doodle Dandy
Of your post-racial
American idol
Of your Jay Z
And Don King
Of your only
In America
Can I be
So poor
Yet dream
Of becoming
So
Rich
Oh America
Take me with you
Make me an offer
I can't refuse
Beat me
Til I believe
Til I fall

To my knees
Till my eyes and teeth
Bleed
To sing
Of thee
Oh soldier
High on that blood rush
That bloodlust
Off all that American dreams
Are made of
All made
To kill
For that
To rape
For flags
Carve that face
To the sides of mountains
Oh captain
My captain
They will grow in your shadows
They will bleed
For you anthems
Old pirate
Come
To rob them
Come
To kill prophets
Born
Of the red flare of rockets

They will take their hearts in their hands
Press your lies to their lips
Fill their lungs with your hymns
Never knowing the histories
That bound them to singing
Over amber waves of chains
As they danced on bones
Drunk off graves
For the land
Of the free
And the home
Of the brave
Oh say
Can you see it?

Naming Practices

El Pueblo
Mexicano
Bracero
La gente
El Norte
First
Second
Third
Generation
Mexican
Unamerican
A class apart
They pulled children from a classroom
And put 'em in a barn
What are you teaching us?
Unassimilated
Brown babies
Half-bred
Indian
Demographic threat
Hostile
To Western Civilization
You say we preach nothing but hate and resentment
But all you ever taught us was shame and self-loathing
You are unfit to teach children
What is known today as ethnic studies

Will tomorrow be science and mathematics
There is strength in numbers
There is power in the naming

Ernie

You know the truth is
There was just so much pain
Anger, resentment
Before and after him
Up and down both sides
His family lineage
Rage
Violence
Addiction
And since you can't fix
What you won't admit
The hardships
Just left him heartless
'Cause he never talked about any of that shit
Shit, Ernie was a mess
Hypocritical, judgmental
Unforgiving and ungrateful
Vindictive
Slow to apologize
Quick to vengeance
Devil's advocate
Casual bigot
No excuses
Man was who he was
A liar
A cheat

Petty thief
Hurt everyone who got near him
Did some time once
Got locked up
For a good long stretch
Ernie never liked to talk about
Bruised knuckles
Paper thin red palms
If not for the cops
His liver might have killed him
Elbows and knees
Knives and liquor
Ernie was a fighting man
Ernie was an angry violent man
Last put on trial
Not before a jury of his peers
But for a TV audience
Police shooting
News at six
Unarmed ex-convict
Gunned down right alongside his demons
Look into this mugshot
Tell me can you see them
Truth is
I would never write this shit
Ernie is fiction
But there are millions just like him
And we need not be angels
To be seen as human

Life is hard enough
Without spitting on death
Fuck the police
And all who enable them

Calilibre

Part one:

This how we begin
This is warmth in the night
Deny
Deflect
Discredit
This is prayer
This is practice
Cover your ears
Close your eyes
These are the lies
That keep things whole
As the far-white
Wraps its fist
In the scowl and spit
Of a hate speech candidate
Proud Boy President
Predator-in-Chief
Open eugenicist
The so-called
Self-appointed
Establishment
Liberal Left
Sit on the fence
Then

Scour the earth
For magic ballot theories
Each
More ridiculous than the next
Couldn't've been racism
Couldn't've be bigotry
Couldn't've been hatred
Couldn't've be misogyny
Couldn't've been the wall
Couldn't've been the ban
Couldn't've been David Duke
Couldn't've been the grab
Couldn't've been anti-blackness
Fear of Muslims
Bad hombres
Or nasty women
Couldn't've been anything this beast
Said or did
On its way to the oval office
No
It was trade
It was
Economic insecurity
It was dissatisfaction with the status quo
It was fear
Of the unknown
It was cultural anxiety
Your fault really
It was the sound of your name

It was the tone of your face
It was a cry
In the night
It was the heartland
The fatherland
Middle America
The real America
Not
You
Waking up
In a country
It did not recognize
It was the bald eagle
Soaring high
Free and victorious
Over all this political correctness
It was a great awakening
A call to greatness
America
Back with a vengeance
It was your insistence
On living here
That made
All these good
Decent
Hard-working people
Vote
For a Klansman
In the aftermath

Of the electoral college
Dropping agent orange upon us
Bernie Panders saw fit
To defend racists
As not racist
Then in practically the next breath
Condemn
An entire generation of Latinas
Telling them
Their lives
Their hopes
Their dreams
Their aspirations
Amounted to no more
Than
Mere identity politics
Why not better
To focus
On the unique pain and abandonment
Of a so-called white working class
Fuck that
Meanwhile
A noted midwest historian
So-called man of the Left
Who still sees US history
As moving east to west
Sees fit to laugh
When I tell him
That the only way to truly understand the current state of

California politics
Is through the lens
Of demographic shift
Knowing nothing of this land
Its history
Its people
Its geography
He only knows
Through closed eyes
And covered ears
That I place
Far too much emphasis
On my existence
That I make politics
Out of feelings
That I am taking all of this
Way
Too personally
But I say this
In a state
That twice elected Pete Wilson
And voted in Nixon and Reagan
Every chance that it got
The browning of California
Has made all the difference
And if a fascist
Begins a political campaign
Calling Mexicans
Drug dealers and rapists

Then it is a matter
Of historic necessity
Destiny
Inevitability
That Califas will lead the resistance
So smile now cry later
You smug motherfucker
'Cause you don't get it
But you will

Part Two:

The Bear Republic
Birthplace of the silver screen
The Gold Rush
And eugenics
Site of Spanish conquest
Lynching Mexicans
Indian auctions
Zyclon b on the border
There are bodies buried
In the parking lot
Of the California mission
Burned codices
Stolen legacy
Forbidden history
Over lands
Lost in battles
Now long forgotten

Twenty-Sixteen
Set the scene
The real MAGAs of Silicon Valley
Versus Sal Si Puedes
The Battle of San José
As the eagle over serpent
Waved
Over the bloodied beaten
Egg-battered faces
Of these fallen racists
As they fled in disgrace
Their triggered eyes
Their bullet minds
Already set their sights
On next day's
Vengeance narrative
Well-prepared
Because it never changes
Mayhem
Riots
Lawless
Violent
Merciless
Savages
Mexican flags
Property damage
Trump used it as evidence
Clinton and Sanders
Denounced it

And the so-called
Liberals and conservatives
Debated the acceptable parameters
Of legitimate protest
Fuck them
The red hats are right
These MAGAS are right
We will rip the shirts from their back
If we do not like what it says
Cinco de Mayo
The candidate
Of an alleged
Lesser white supremacy
Protected by armored cars
And beasts on horseback
Slogan drenched
Cliched speech in hand
Descended upon the campus
East Los Angeles
Hillary Clinton
In full condescension
Here to bidi bidi bom bom
Her way into the hearts and minds
Of people
She had asked
To emoji tweet
Autobiographies
Of debt and despair
Taco bowl engagement

And the flags
The flags of the continent flew
South and Central America
Pan Africa
Marxistas
Mechistas
To the chants of
You killed Berta
Murderer
You murdered her
Banners and placards
Raised against yankee imperialism
To chants of "Chale Hillary"
Til just minutes in
The career politician
Self-styled abuela
Turned and fled
Because this has never been
About the burning bridges
And towers
The war cry
Of the democratic vote
Those sell-outs in Sacramento
Their white party bosses
Their rich white donors
Vendido-ragoisa
Or whoever
A so-called
Demographic

Ticking time bomb
Cannot negate
A class struggle to be won
Fuck them all

Part three:

Later that night
I recalled the incident
To a so-called white progressive
Who saw fit to laugh
Scratch his head
Look perplexed
Then finally ask
"So they were marching against Hillary?"
I said, "hell yeah"
He said
"Were they marching for Trump?"
I said, "Fuck no"
He asked, "Were they marching for Bernie?"
I said, "Some but not most"
He asked
"Well, then who are they for?"
I said, "Themselves"
He said, "I don't get it"
I said, "Smile now, cry later"
Calilibre

A Tradition of Fodder

Depression era
Chamber of commerce says
Mass expulsion government
Can't even keep a white man fed
Mexicans keep moving
Field to cannery
Coal to furnace
Hand to mouth
Suffer this silence
Serve this country
This land you had better love
Take hold of the arsenal of democracy
Check the stats
POWs missing in action
Aztlan to Vietnam
That pushout rate will bury you
And high in the center of town
That flag
And all that it represents
Some kind of tradition in these parts
And the ROTC runs the high school campus
And Donald Trump is president

Chicano in Liverpool

The sun never set on such bullshit
I did not come to the United Kingdom
Only to find the United States
And yet
Here I stand
Hailing a cab
In the former slaveport of Liverpool
Driver's shirt reading
"The original border patrol"
Picturing the Texas Rangers
Rifles in hand
And yet
A drunken UKIP hooligan
Breathing down the back of my neck
You are not from here
"Are you?"
"Are you?"
"You don't belong here"
"Do you?"
"Do you?"
Man fuck you

Good Money

Law and enforcement
Commerce and displacement
Debasement
Operations and programs
The making
Of braceros and wetbacks
Citizens and aliens
Dreamers and bad hombres
The breaking of the treaty
Hernandez, La Migra
Lawful American
Enemy of the people
Says his job patriotic
Never political
An honest wage
For an honest day
But in moments of silence
Views himself
As a man divided
Even his reflections
Are dishonest
Even his truths
Holds secrets
Foot soldier of conquest
This world will be a better place
Once you're thrown into that grave

"Why would you protest a coffee shop?"
"What could you possibly have against art?"
"My grandma still lives in those apartments
You saying I don't love my abuela?"
Ortega
Family friendly homegrown neighborhood developer
Knows which hands to shake
Which promises to break
And which
To leave alone
Friend to
Flipsters and startups
Gastropubs and charters
The wagon trail and Wells Fargo
Barrio guide
Of a wasteland of vacant lots
At least that's how he sells it
Opportunist
Translator
Traitor
Vendido
Pathfinder
Collaborator
And there are words
Worse for you still
They said this was hard
But
It was never hard for you
Lecture hall

Eager white faces
Name and complexion
Stamps the passport
To imagination
Step inside it
Find yourself in it
Live in debasement
Solis
Seller of stories
Master of the fine arts
You heard this was hard
But high art
Was never hard for you
Soar
Beyond cynicism
Sing of limbs
Severed in the river
That belonged to no one
Intoxicate them
With the taste of danger
Light their imagination
With tales of coyotes
Cartels
Dead children
And a cast of victims
And villains
That died so brown
They were barely even human
Sell those people

Your people
Our people
And how lucky
They all are
Not to be them
You heard this was hard
But who would know better than you
An MFA is only as good as you work it
Now go tell those people what they came to hear
They pay good money for that shit

Here is a Nation

Here is a nation
Packaged complete
Police
Escort
Skinheads
And hooded Klansmen
To march hate
Down public streets
While those very
Same police
Quotas to meet
Cannon fire
On black boys
In hoodies
And Mexican kids
With
Shaved heads
They are killing our kids
While half the nation
Applauds
In the homeland's defense
Because they think
They think
That a white woman's purse
Has more value
Than a black or brown boy's life

Here is a nation
Hell bent
One percent
Genocide
Pipeline
From underfunded schools
To overcrowded prisons
Newt Gingrich our kids
Say they ain't fit
For nothing
But life in
And out of the system
Stripped of innocence
Guilt by birth certificate
Students
Quotas
Before
Children
Children
Suspects
Before students
Young girls
Whores
Before victims
Here is a nation
That eats its young
This is not a democracy
This is not a republic
This is an open-air prison

An industrial-scale plantation
Anything
And
Everything
You have ever gotten
From this system
Has been a mathematical assessment
A calculated equation
Set to the algorithm
Of the cost of doing business
Keep your hands moving
Stomach consuming
Mind functioning
Within the narrow confines
Of your job description
Blood soaked country
Forged in genocide
Built on slavery
By a den of thieves
Posing as messiah
The constitution
Thomas Jefferson
Jefferson Davis
White Jesus
Western civilization
Civilizing mission
Mission accomplished
Manifest Destiny
American exceptionalism

Peculiar institution
Institutionalized racism
Declaration
To plantation
Anthem
To slave ship
The bicentennial
And back
To the slave whip
At the feet
Of Lady Liberty
To the dirt poor
Dead tired
Huddled child
Labor driven
Pauper field
Tenements
Of Ellis Island
To Arizona's
Blood red
Coyote trails
Traffic
In brown flesh
Brick by brick
Grave by grave
Inch by inch
Slave by slave
Here is a nation
There are its chains

Keep you in place

Watchtower

Overseer

Injun killer

Union bust

McCarthyism

Patriot act

Acting in

Interest of

National defense

Which of you

Would stand against it?

Witch-hunt for whistle blown

"Who said that?"

"Who did that?"

Which side

"Are you on?"

Here is the firing squad

That killed Metacomet

That killed Tecumseh

That killed Joaquin Murrieta

That killed John Brown

That killed Nat Turner

The killed the Rosenbergs

Sacco and Vanzetti

Malcolm X and Martin Luther King

Killed Ruben Salazar

Killed Fred Hampton

That will continue to kill

In much the same fashion
Here are the blood-soaked fields
That claimed the life of
Andy Lopez
Brisenia Flores
Susy Peña
Mike Brown
Latasha Harlins
Trayvon Martin
Half the nation applauded
Here is that nation
This is not a democracy
This is not a republic
This is the state of the union
They are killing our children
We are at war
And this is a call to arms

El Sereno

I was born
On the eastside of Los Angeles
Across the tracks
From abandoned steel
An industrial petrified forest
Across the steps
A giant green tarp
Protected customers
And gossipers
Our abuelitas
From rays of sun
And the bombs of birds
They spoke Spanish
Sold mangos
Papayas
And cherries
My favorite
As a child
I could never quite
Make the connection
Between the broken
And empty bottles
Across the steps
And the broken and empty men
Poured out the rust factories
From across the tracks

So
My cousins and I
Would gather and throw
Rocks of dirt
As hard as we could
Aimed directly for the head
And they would yell
Something like
What do you damn kids know
About life?
And we would yell back
Take that drunks!
That was messed up
But that's just the way it was
Growing up where Valley
Goes up and over
To meet Soto
El Sereno
1950s
My mother's father
A technician
By trade
By birth
A prince among men
In a backwards kingdom
That held him back
Treated him different
For the radiance
Of his beautiful

Brown skin
There is hard fought genius
In me
Older than my mother's womb
December 18th, 1981
After months
Of fear and absence
My father makes his return
My aunt moves to protect
Hospital bed
She does not want to see you
You know what you did
It would be best
If you just left
My mother
Holds her newborn
Her only begotten son
Half her creation
There is a pain in me
Older than my father's blood
As a child
I could never quite make the connection
Between
His fingers around my throat
And the anguish
In his chest
A suffering
Older than my father's bones
 His father's whiskey

His grandfather's short temper
Long lived legacy
To time history does not care
To remember
Because beatings
Are not fit for scrapbooks
And genealogies of shame
Rarely make their way
To the oral tradition
Of campfire
There is a burning
In my heart
That time
Cannot trace
Moved out of my father's
The suburbs treated me different
One day
In the workforce
I told my boss
"Last night
I met
A woman
Beautiful
Intelligent"
Asks where at
"Boyle Heights"
"Where's that?"
"Eastside of Los Angeles"
Asks

Incredulous
"You meant an intelligent woman
In East Los Angeles?"
I wanted to slap
The manifest destiny
Out of his smirk
Beat the cavalry
Off his name badge
But needing a paycheck
I stood
In the weakness
Of silence
The pain and anguish
Of generations
Long past
Alive and sickened
In my chest
There is a shame
Attempted upon us
Older than the tongues
Of bigots
Walked off job
Marched through lot
Fist up for the cause
'Cause in a world
That has told us no
That has told us different
I have chosen yes
Yes

I am Chicano
Yes
Mexicano
Yes
Indigenous
Yes
I brown skin
And bleed red
Yes
Unafraid and unashamed
Of my passion
My potential
My intelligence
Yes
The fire in my chest
Look into my eyes
And you can feel
Its strength
And yes
As a matter of fact
Some of the most radiant
Talented
Gifted
Beautiful
Intelligent
Women
I have ever met
Reside
On the eastside

Of Los Angeles
Just across the steps
From the streets
Where I was born
Yes
I am all of this and more
I like you
Am made of stars
You like me
So full of pain
Are brimming with genius
Listen to no one
Who would make you feel different

Once Upon a Go Back to Mexico

"You know, who knows man?"
I mean who really fucking knows
Where it all began
Where the time goes
Where the money went
How this shit gets made
Who runs the board
Who calls the shots
And who gets played
See I am Mexican
Mexican-American
Chicano US born and raised
So you know what comes next
Dirty lazy stupid
Beaner wetback spic
You already know how the story begins
How else but with
Once upon a go back to Mexico
"Must've been about five or six
Sometimes these things happen a little sooner than expected
Sorry kid
That's just the way that it is
Seems like you're gonna have to make a decision
Think quick
Don't flinch

Thumbs out
Clench your fist now
Or forever hold your tongue
See I was born in eighty-one
Which makes me young Gen X
Or old Millennial
Shit, I don't know
Sometimes it seems like my birthright
Is just more questions than answers
What I do know is this
Something terrible happened
Around four hundred and eighty-nine years before I was born
And my life, well, it just hasn't been the same since
See, what you call microaggressions
I call miniconquests
See them by the water cooler
Sailing in my mind dressed like
John Smith, Hernán Cortés
Chest plates and muskets
Shoe buckles and loaded questions
Office eugenics, pointed statements like
"When Polk took Mexico City, he should have taken the whole
thing"
Or
All illegals are diseased
"You were born here, so why are you offended?"
And if I acted like I did when I was a kid
Shit, you already know what would happen
But I was never one to repent or confess

'Cause I was not born to be forgiven

Not here, not now, not by them,

Saw a man run for President

Said I saw a man run for President

Then heard a rainbow coalition of friends debate

Whether calling Mexicans drug dealers and rapists was racist
or populist

Then demand a discussion, a reflection and some nuance

Why couldn't I feel the pain of people who felt nothing but
hate for mine

And all I could do was reflect upon my life and ask myself why

'Cause sometimes it seems like the more I think

The less I know

And the more I speak

The worse it gets

And even when ready to fight

We don't know what the hell we are talking about

Our mouths just running

Muttering something about a nation of immigrants

Always trying to make sense of our lives with images not our
own

Just some second-hand bootleg history

Written for us to serve them

'Cause the real power lies not in the pursuit

Of the answer

But in the posing of the question

'Cause sometimes it seems like someone is always trying to
convince me of something

Like there are things they don't want us to see

Like they are manipulating reality
Some nights I drive this city
And see nothing but brown faces
Then go back inside turn on the television
I don't see them till I go out again
'Cause sometimes it seems like we're here but we are not
Like they want to blame us
And not allow a response
Like no part of this culture is ours
Like perpetually foreign
Like an apartheid state of mind
Where they capture the imagination to prevent the future from
being born
Like the Mexican-American War never ended
And every billboard in the city of Los Angeles
Is screaming some white savior shrouded in penance or revolt
But everybody knows
Everybody knows Jesus and Joker
And both of them are Mexican
Everybody already knows how this story ends America
What do you get?
What do you get when you steal half a nation then oppress its
descendants?
I'll tell you what you get
You get what you fucking deserve

Seditious (An Ode to Self)

I declare this poem Seditious
An ode to my motherfucking self
A tribute to my travels
And a toast upon my name
I send no regard
To that old life set adrift
I crack the bottle bon voyage
On the maiden voyage
Of the good ship
Go fuck yourselves
I sing the miles distance
Put between me and those insignificant retail racists who used
to hold my check this out
Speaking of my success
Spoken at something like
A hundred college campuses
Three continents
My life enshrined in archives
My opinion solicited by the Associated Press
I have walked the Malecón
And strolled the castles of Cambridge
But it's like I always say
Live
And let those Goddamn racists mark out their days
Only to be buried in practically unmarked graves
With their names written on them
And I know that sounds elitist

But I don't give a fuck
'Cause nobody does
I have eaten Finnish pancakes in Thunder Bay Canada
And if you're ever out there
If you ever get the chance
Check out the saunas
But you won't
'Cause you can't
'Cause you suck
Fuck you
Lousy Goddamn racist fucks

Kingdom of Cages

Los Angeles, city of pigs
Kingdom of cages
Database, the Fuhrman tapes, the Ayres report
Darryl Gates, Tom Bradley, Lee Baca, Willie Parker
The red lines, red squads, ramparts, Rodney King
The thin blue line on an all-white jury
Murderous metropolis that kills for appearances
Chicano Moratorium, eighty-four Olympics
CRASH, the battering ram
Crack the CIA
Twin towers, Operation Hammer, Safe city
La Loma, Bishop, Palo Verde, Arcadia
Los Angeles is a city designed to be divided
Postcard paradise, gentleman's apartheid
Service and protection, 41st and central
SWAT, Watts, Sleepy Lagoon
Open shop, open season
The killer of children, take the shot
They were sworn to protect
As we serve as their moving targets, their bleeding borders
Their open frontiers, the neighborhood threat
As they shoot us as we run
As they shoot us as we run
As they shoot us as we run
As they shoot us as we run
As they shoot us as we run

As they shoot us as we run

As they shoot us as we run

As they shoot us as we run

As they shoot us as we run

As they shoot us as we run

As they shoot us as we run

As they shoot us as we run

Jessie Romero was fourteen years old

When murdered by the LAPD

Los Angeles, city of pigs, kingdom of cages

Mowing Leaves of Grass

I am the as yet written vengeance of Elvira Valdez
The best laid plans of Modesta
The reckoning of Santa Cruz
San Ysidro
Bisbee
Chandler
Porvenir
The blood sweat and tears
Of all that I refuse to forget
I am that unpaid debt
No sidekick
No subplot
No mascot
No ethnic study
The universe I embody
The ground above me
The sky beneath my feet
Marching las calles
Y las estrellas
Through circular calendars
Sleep dealing
Siqueiros y Rivera
Past the past
The future
In the present
In Lak'ech

All at once
'Cause in this moment
I am you
And you are me
And we
Are two clenched fists
That still lit fire
Sacred kept
The final breath
Of the so-called
Last fighting Aztec
Laughing in the face of death
The blade of el pachuco
Guarding the temple steps
The strength of memory
The promise of tomorrow
Yo soy Chicano
Y Chicano soy
Y adonde me lleves
El Chicano voy
They want you to think this is important
Critical
To your rehabilitation
For the way in which you entered this world
Read Thomas Jefferson
Or else you'll get pregnant
Standards and practices
Curriculum and instruction
And you the product

Of public education
Do not interrupt
Or you'll be led cuffed
Face-first
Into pavement
Like
Your father
Your grandfather
Your mother
Your nina
Your tios
Til you learn your lesson
It's not personal
It's all you people
So don't get mad
Don't be hurt
And don't make this political
This is economic
Objective
The law of self-interest
If we let you in
What will become
Of the canon
The classics, Alexander and Napoleon
Who will shelve
The wit and wisdom
Of Ben Franklin
Shelly
Shakespeare

Chaucer
Walt Whitman
From the
Paumanok
Starting
What has
Miserable
Inefficient Mexico
To do with the great mission
The new world
The noble race
You fought
You lost
You don't get to define this
This isn't racism
It's providence
Progress
And god willing
You filthy mongrels
It is just the way it is
I look at you
And I don't see color
I see labor
I see law and order
Cops and robbers
Guards and convicts
Institutions of correction
Schools that look like prisons
Caged apartments

Where the cost of living
The cost of being
Brown
Is as high
As wage theft
And the rent
Forget
Your savage tongue
I will teach you
This robust
American love
Spoon feed you spics
Freedom of speech
Til you learn
To take a joke
And speak to authority
I will show you
Who you are
In a book
And you will believe it
'Cause I said it
And now you read it
And who are you
To question
The canon the classics
Lowry
Kerouac
Walk out
On the great white brilliance

Of Wilson

Garfield

Roosevelt

Lincoln

Now listen 'cause

'Cause this is important

The universe

Is a muralist

The cosmos

Our self-portrait

Starring

A curandera

A danzante

A poet laureate

A stylist

A mechanic

The barrio dandy

Cruising the rings of Saturn

To the travel tips of Torres

Carrasco tearing

Down the curtain

On union station

Joaquin returning

Triumphant

Marching

Through the halls of Tucson

Mowing down leaves of grass

Fuck Walt Whitman

This is

An Art Laboe
Dedication
To
Frida
Selena
Cantinflas
Luis Rodriguez
Valdez
The Mighty Quinn
Sandra
Sor Juana
Anzaldúa
To all that we are
And all we have been
Through lifelines
And timelines
Galaxies and dimensions
Of pain pride and resistance
And gothic
Are the solar showers
In the days of living music
When the people of the sun
Are dancing to the tune of Valenzuela
And la luna
Was a calvera
As the ancestors
Welcomed in the future
Through circular calendars
Where I am you

And you are me
Sitting at a desk
Looking to the stars
Searching for the end
To a poem
That never began
That always was
And forever shall be

Custers

Custers and Confederates
Crusaders and little Davy Crocketts
Pick up their politics
From the Alamo's gift shop
Sunday Knights of Columbus
And Monday morning lynch mobs
Not all Nazis hit the street
Not all Klan wash their own sheets
The keyboard cavalry sit comfortably
Behind, "How's that racist?"
"Let's try to stay objective"
And the white to free speech
Fuck your words
Fuck your hat
Fuck your leader
Fuck his tan
Fuck a registry
Fuck the ban
Fuck your law
Fuck your order
Fuck your wall
Fuck your border
Fuck you Chachi
And fuck Ann Coulter
Taco trucks every corner
"Fuck some nuance

I speak plain

Fuck America

It was never great

Fuck Hulk Hogan

And fuck John Wayne

Ffffuuuuuuuuuuuuuucccckkkkk

Latinos for Trump

Gusanos

Cristeros

Vendidos

You need to look in the mirror

'Cause you got some shit confused

'Cause when they said build a wall

Well they meant your ass too

So fuck lil Marco

And chinga la Ted Cruz

Fuck Paul Ryan

Fuck Mike Pence

Fuck Mad Dog

War is not defense

Fuck Betsy

Fuck Perry

Fuck Kayne

Fuck Rudy

Fuck Ivanka

Fuck Melania

Fuck Eric

Fuck Jared

Fuck Donny Junior

Fuck the Mercers
Fuck Huckabee Sanders
Fuck Miller
Fuck Spencer
Fuck Spicer
Fuck Kris Kobach
Fuck Michael Savage
Fuck Lou Dobbs
And fuck Steve Bannon
Fuck Rex Tillerson
Fuck Jeff Sessions
And fuck you Ben Carson
You know damn well those were slave ships
Fuck Donald Trump
Fuck his whole crew
And if you're down with Donald Trump
Well then
Fuck
You
Too
Little fucking Custers

Made in the USA
Las Vegas, NV
29 April 2024

89310232R00080